CAREER AS A
POLICE DETECTIVE

CRIMINAL INVESTIGATOR

NO CAREER HAS BEEN MORE ROMANTICIZED in novels, television shows, and movies than that of a police detective. The real world of criminal investigation has little in common with the cool, fast-paced, slick-talking fictional version everyone has become so familiar with. Sometimes the job is dangerous and heart pounding, but you do not spend most of your time tailing criminals to exotic parts of the world to unravel a mystery loaded with international intrigue. For most criminal investigators, the work involves solving crimes much closer to home by tirelessly piecing together shreds of evidence that lead them to a suspect.

You will be doing lots of legwork and scouring the evidence over and over again until something new pops out at you. The job takes courage, but it takes even more patience. Unlike the television version of a day in the life of some police detectives, crimes are never solved in an hour.

In addition, most criminal investigators would love nothing more than to focus all their attention on one case until it is solved. That never happens. Real police detectives work on numerous cases at one time and often bemoan the fact that they cannot devote more time to a particular case. Police detectives do go out on the road. They shadow suspects, interview witnesses, follow clues, reinvestigate the crime scene, and gather evidence.

Unlike uniformed police officers, criminal investigators usually work in suits and ties. Some wear more casual attire, working undercover to infiltrate criminal operations, get close to suspects, and learn about criminal activities firsthand before making an arrest.

This career entails a great deal of paperwork, including the careful handling and meticulous categorizing of evidence. Police detectives gather evidence that is often needed during a trial so a prosecutor can successfully make a case against the offenders.

Police detectives are charged with the awesome responsibility of apprehending the person who committed a crime. If a hardworking detective does not break the case, chances are the crime will never be solved. That is why the best detectives never give up on a case. They are always thinking about it, viewing it from different angles, searching for new clues, and canvassing a neighborhood looking for witnesses who saw something but never came forward.

No matter how simple a case may seem, this job is never easy. If you love a good mystery and are willing to follow it through all its twists and turns, wherever it leads, being a criminal investigator may be the career for you.

WHAT YOU CAN DO NOW

MANY COMMUNITIES HAVE POLICE explorer posts, which are an offshoot of the Boy Scouts of America. These explorer posts are open to both boys and girls, generally ages 14 to 20. Explorer posts give you insight into what it is like to be a police officer. You will meet and talk with real police officers, as well as detectives, and do ride-alongs. It is a good opportunity to get a behind-the-scenes look at the career and see if law enforcement is the right job for you.

Stay in shape or get into shape. A police detective's job is physically demanding. Creating a practical workout routine and developing the discipline to stick with it will help you in this job throughout your career.

Learn to be observant. Detectives notice things that other people overlook. You would be surprised how many people see something but do not pay attention to what they are looking at. Savvy detectives not only see and remember what went on, but they pick up nuances that other people completely miss. Recall what color shirt your friend was wearing today? A good detective would.

HISTORY OF THE CAREER

ONE OF THE FIRST POLICE DETECTIVES, known for his prowess in solving baffling crimes, actually led a life of mystery before donning a badge. Eugene Francois Vidocq was himself a criminal as a young man! Born in 1775 in Arras, France, Vidocq turned to a life of crime and mayhem when he was eighteen. He was in and out of prison throughout France for a variety of offenses until the age of 34. However, Vidocq rarely spent much time in prison after being arrested because he was clever and a master of disguise. He kept figuring out ways to escape from prison, and repeatedly eluded capture.

In 1809, tired of life on the run, Vidocq brazenly approached John Henry, the chief of the Criminal Department in Paris, with a proposition. In exchange for amnesty for all his crimes, Vidocq offered to become a police informant. The once-daring criminal knew all the crooks in France and proved to be an extremely valuable resource to French police officials. He gave them information on crimes that had gone unsolved for years, and even about crimes that were being planned.

By 1811, Vidocq had organized a team of civilian, plainclothes, undercover detectives – all former criminals – who combed Paris for hardened lawbreakers. Vidcoq believed that reformed criminals made the best detectives because they were streetwise and knew the inner workings of the underworld.

Vidocq's crew of crime fighters was called the Sûreté, French for security, and became an official arm of the police in 1812. By 1820, Vidocq's band of detectives, which started out with just four men, had grown to 28 men and had reduced crime in Paris by 40 percent. Now known as La Sûreté Nationale, the detective unit started by Vidocq served as the model for law enforcement organizations around the world, including England's renowned Scotland Yard and the FBI in the United States.

England's criminal element had a hand in helping start that nation's first centralized detective bureau in 1842. However, unlike Vidocq, these criminals did not come forward to help solve crime. Rather, they exploited Greater London's Metropolitan Police Department's inability to successfully apprehend the culprits. A series of botched investigations by constables, including the mishandling of a gruesome murder in April 1842, made the Metropolitan Police Department the focus of harsh criticism from both the public and the press. Bowing to the public outcry and pressure from the press for competent and effective police investigations, the Metropolitan Police Department started a detective bureau. The bureau would handle not only murder investigations, but fraud and theft cases as well.

In the United States, the Boston Police Department was suffering from much the same fate as London's Metropolitan police force. In 1846, Albert Tirrell was charged by Boston police with murdering his mistress. It was considered an open-and-shut case. But a jury found Tirrell not guilty of the crime, blaming the Boston police for not collecting enough evidence to convict the man. Outraged by the outcome of the trial, Boston's newly elected mayor, Josiah Quincy Jr. took a cue from England and started a detective bureau in the Boston Police Department. It was the first police unit in the United States exclusively devoted to investigating crimes and properly securing evidence. The bureau had a staff of four detectives to start off with. That was enough, as it turned out. Early successes of the detective bureau were covered by the press, and these sleuths began to gain credibility in the eyes of the public and their peers in the police department.

Meanwhile, other big cities, like Chicago, Detroit, Philadelphia, and New York, added detective bureaus, following Boston's example. In 1849, Chicago hired its first police detective, Allan Pinkerton. Pinkerton went on to become a renowned police detective as well as a celebrated private detective.

As more major cities adopted the concept of police detective bureaus, the profession got a major boost from science and technology. In the late 1800s, police detectives increasingly began to rely on fingerprints to help solve criminal cases. Then, at the turn of the 20th century, they started employing ballistics on a regular basis to identify weapons used in crimes. All this legitimized the work of criminal investigators.

When US Attorney General Charles Bonaparte created an agency made up exclusively of sleuths to investigate federal crimes, detective work got national respect and attention in the United States. That agency, first known as the Bureau of Investigation, changed its name to the Federal Bureau of Investigation (FBI) in 1935.

Through the decades that followed, criminal investigation improved with each new forensic breakthrough. The field was also bolstered by new training methods that honed the investigative skills of investigators. Today, police detectives and criminal investigators are considered law enforcement's most elite crime fighters.

WHERE YOU WILL WORK

WITH APPROXIMATELY 15,400 LOCAL police and sheriff's departments in the United States, there are plenty of places for aspiring criminal investigators to work. Not all these departments have a detective on the force, but a majority of them do, and most have well-staffed detective bureaus.

Police departments are located in large and small urban, suburban, and rural municipalities. Sheriff's officers are usually county-based. In addition, there are 50 state police departments across the country, and more than 50 federal law enforcement agencies, like the US Park Police and the US Secret Service. All hire criminal investigators.

For the most part, police departments in small municipalities run their entire operation out of one main headquarters building, usually located in a municipal complex. From that headquarters, police, including detectives, are dispatched. Administrative staff work from the headquarters, and police reports and records are kept there as well. Also in the headquarters building are the evidence room – where evidence concerning ongoing and past police investigations is stored – and holding cells.

Big cities, like New York, Boston, Chicago, and Detroit, have a headquarters that serves as the law enforcement agency's nerve center and houses various police operations, records, and administrative staff. In these big cities, where there is much ground to cover, territory is divided into precincts, each with a local precinct house. This puts police personnel right in the middle of a neighborhood, making it easier for them to respond to calls rapidly.

Some county law enforcement agencies, with very large areas to cover, use regional, district, or satellite offices to accomplish their mission. State police have their headquarters in the state's capital city, with regional barracks throughout that state. Federal agencies are headquartered in Washington, DC and have district offices in large metropolitan areas nationwide.

Your work environment is determined by the municipality where you are a police detective. You may probe criminal activity in the expanses of rural America; the hustle, bustle, congestion, and blight of the inner city; or a serene suburban setting. State and federal criminal investigators may work in any of these environments, depending on where their assignment takes them.

You will not be spending much time behind a desk. During most of your day, you will be out on the road at crime scenes, interviewing witnesses, and tracking down criminals. A crime can occur anywhere. You never know where you will be sent to conduct an investigation. It might be an office building, a home, or an open field. Crime scenes are never a pleasant place to work. They are always surrounded by chaos and tumult. However, police detectives and criminal investigators spend hours, sometimes days, at these scenes, trying to determine exactly how a crime was committed and collecting evidence.

Police detectives do not want to inconvenience witnesses who are cooperating with an investigation, so detectives visit these people at their places of business, at home, or anywhere the witness is comfortable talking about the incident. You follow suspects wherever their tracks lead you, whether it is the next town over or around the world.

THE WORK YOU WILL DO

ANYTHING FOUND AT A CRIME SCENE – no matter how large or how small – could be the piece of evidence that unlocks the mystery. Seemingly meaningless scribbles on a pad, an abandoned car, a strand of fiber hardly noticed by the naked eye could all be clues that can crack a case.

Once a crime is committed, your first priority is to get to the crime scene. To the untrained person, that scene is just a hectic, disorderly mess. To the police detective, a crime scene is a source of key evidence, containing the answer to many questions, including what happened and who did it.

Most detectives do not dig into the scene of the crime, searching for evidence, immediately. They take a moment to carefully observe the entire area and try to imagine what might have happened. Slowly, they begin to examine objects that might hold a key to unraveling the case. Armed robberies, assaults, murders, auto thefts, break-ins, even white collar crimes, all have crime scenes with evidence that allows criminal investigators to start solving the crime and building a case.

Usually, before anything is disturbed, an investigator has a police photographer take pictures of the area where the crime was committed. The detective oversees all the picture taking. There might be hundreds of still pictures taken. Video is also used to record how the crime scene originally looked. Once all the evidence is removed and the crime scene cleaned, these visuals will be the only links detectives have to how the area looked when police first arrived.

Sketches and diagrams of the layout of the building or the room where the crime took place may also be hand drawn by police artists under the direction of the lead detective on the case. As the photograph session is proceeding and any drawings are being made, detectives are taking notes about the crime scene.

Careful note taking is an ongoing process throughout the investigation. These notes will be invaluable to you, especially since you will most likely be handling more than one case at a time. Notes have to be orderly and well written, and include anything that you might want to look back on at a later time. Every detail must be recorded; nothing can be left to memory alone, because an important element of the case may be forgotten or overlooked.

Once all the visuals have been recorded and you have completed your notes on what the crime scene looked like when you first saw it, you begin collecting the evidence. This involves the painstaking process of combing through the location where the crime took place and removing anything that might have the slightest connection with the case. Mud, flower petals, broken pieces of glass, hair, dust – the most seemingly insignificant item can become your biggest lead. Each item must be bagged or placed in a container, marked by you, and preserved. Preservation is extremely important. The integrity of the evidence cannot be compromised by permitting it to become degraded or contaminated.

Sometimes evidence, like fingerprints, can be processed right at the crime scene. Other evidence, like hair samples, has to be taken to the laboratory to be analyzed. Large police departments and law enforcement agencies have their own crime labs with forensic experts on staff, but smaller departments have to send out certain evidence collected at the crime scene, like blood, hair, and fiber samples, to an outside laboratory to be examined.

Many detectives visit the laboratories, to speak with the forensic experts who examined the evidence, seeking their input on what they saw and their thoughts on the case. In a murder case, a detective might want to talk to the medical examiner who did the autopsy on the victim. Sometimes medical examiners can give criminal investigators scientific insights into the death of the victim and the motive of the killer.

One of the most important parts of the job is conducting interviews with victims, witnesses, informants, and anyone else who might have information relating to the crime. Any of these people can help generate leads that might put you on the trail of the culprit.

Though police detectives and criminal investigators do some preliminary interviews with victims and witnesses at the crime scene, more in-depth interviews are conducted at police headquarters a day or two after the crime is committed. Even though it is good to talk to victims and witnesses while the crime is still fresh in their minds, after some time passes, and people think back on the episode, they often remember something that they did not recall in the tumult that followed the incident. In addition, giving victims and witnesses a few days to calm down allows detectives to review their notes and come up with questions they might not have thought of when first interviewing these people.

Interviews are vital to the detection process. It is your job as a police detective and criminal investigator to get victims and witnesses to trust you. People often say, "I already told the police everything I know about what happened," but victims and witnesses may omit something when they are first interviewed that they thought was insignificant. For example, perhaps the victim of a break-in where jewelry was stolen had gone to the jewelry store the day before her house was robbed to pick up a valuable necklace that had been repaired at the store. In the excitement of seeing the expert repair job, the victim put on the necklace. A man in the store at the time walked over, admired the piece of jewelry, showed great interest in it, and commented that it must be very expensive.

The repaired necklace had been in an envelope waiting for pickup. Once the victim took the necklace, the store clerk threw the envelope into a garbage can near the sales counter. The garbage can was easily accessible to the public. The envelope had the victim's name, address, and phone number on it.

In the break-in, the necklace was one of the items stolen. But during her first interview with the police, right after the crime was committed, the victim said nothing about picking up the necklace the day before the break-in.

During the second interview, the victim mentioned that she was especially upset that the necklace had been stolen because she had just had it repaired. She then went into the story about the interest the other customer in the jewelry store had expressed in the necklace. Detectives then had a new lead and a possible suspect.

Informants usually hear about crimes or know when high volumes of valuables are being fenced, and can give police leads on increased criminal activity.

Police detectives and criminal investigators also interrogate suspects. Not every suspect is the person who committed the crime. Once detectives have the name of a suspect, they check the person's background and see if the individual has a criminal record. They do some additional legwork as well.

Following up on the case of the stolen necklace, detectives go to the jewelry store where the necklace was repaired. They question employees about whether they saw anything suspicious when the female victim was in the store, picking up the necklace. No one seems to recall anything untoward, but then one young clerk sheepishly comes forward and says he saw the man in question dip into the garbage can and grab the envelope. The clerk did not want to get anyone in trouble, including his co-worker, who threw the envelope into the trash can. The clerk goes on to say that the man then went outside the store and got on the phone.

After reviewing surveillance tapes recorded at the jewelry store, the clerk points out the man. Other clerks look at the tape as well and one of them recognizes the man as someone who sold some gold to the store in the past. The jewelry store owners require identification from anyone selling gold or silver to them. The man's contact information is on file. Police run a background check on the man and find that he was arrested for petty theft in the past. Investigators are now ready to bring the man in for questioning as a suspect in the case.

Questioning suspects is usually an adversarial process. At first, suspects are not going to admit to anything. Most will talk openly, telling you that they did not commit the crime. Many will have alibis. A suspect's story is not necessarily all lies to start out with, just a series of interwoven events, making it look as if he could not have been involved in committing the crime. These stories sound innocent – more omissions than lies. Your job is to identify the gaps in the story and start demanding specifics. As a suspect begins to fill in the blanks, you can start checking out the facts. This is where the suspect's story will either check out or fall apart. Even if the suspect's story might be crumbling, you still have the job of building your case against that person. You have to establish probable cause, so you can get a judge to issue a search warrant for the suspect's residence, automobile, or place of business to look for any evidence connecting him to the case. Linking evidence found at the crime scene with the suspect is extremely important in building your case. The same is true when it comes to linking evidence found in the suspect's home, car, or office with evidence gathered at the crime scene.

Today's new technology also plays a role in evidence gathering. Phone records and computer files have to be analyzed to see if there is a digital footprint linking the suspect to the crime.

Once you have enough evidence, you make an arrest and charge the suspect with a crime. You forward your findings to prosecutors so the case can make its way through the court system.

For criminal investigators, one of the most unpleasant aspects of the job can be testifying in court. Most police detectives and criminal investigators will be subpoenaed to testify in court at some point in their careers. This is where your case file notes will be necessary, because a majority of cases take months, sometimes more than a year or so, before they are heard in court, and you will not be able to rely on your memory of all the details.

When you do finally testify, defense attorneys will question many of your findings, trying to challenge how you put the evidence together and came to the conclusion that their client did it. If you did your job properly, the jury or judge will see that your investigation is solid. With the support and testimony of other prosecution witnesses, your findings will stand up in court and the suspect will be convicted. You will have accomplished what you started out to do: see justice done.

DETECTIVES TELL THEIR OWN STORIES

I Am a Police Detective in a Small Municipality

"I think the biggest difference between working in a large police detective bureau and a small one is specialization. In a small unit, like this one, we have six detectives and we work whatever cases we are assigned, no matter what the crime is. In other words, we don't have special units that only handle homicide, auto thefts, juvenile crimes, and so forth, as they do in large municipalities.

This is a town of 16,000 people, 20 square miles. Fortunately, we don't have to deal with homicides very often and we have a limited number of major crimes, but we do have our fair share of robberies, auto theft, break-ins, vandalism and other crimes against property, drug-related crimes, and abuse cases, primarily against children and the elderly. All these crimes have to be investigated.

I like working in a small bureau. Having a diverse variety of cases is something that appeals to me. I wake up every day and feel I want to help somebody. I believe every police officer feels that way, or least should.

I never lose sight of the fact that any crime that is committed is a major crime to the victim. There is no small case when somebody has violated your space, your security. It's my goal to solve every case, whether it's just kids doing a prank, a petty thief who goes into someone's yard at night and steals gardening tools, or a vicious assault. Each victim gets my full attention and my best effort.

I track down all the leads and I keep victims updated on the progress of the case. So often people feel there is no one in the system who cares, and I don't want the victims whose cases I get to feel that way. I became a police officer to make a difference and I feel I can really do that in the detective bureau by solving cases and helping victims see justice done.

Piecing together what happened at the crime scene is only part of the job. You also have to try to put together at least a sketchy profile of who this perpetrator is, to get an idea of who and what you are dealing with.

You review unsolved cases over and over again, trying to find some scrap of information you might have missed the first hundred times you looked at the file. You interview anyone in the area surrounding the crime scene who might know something about what happened, even though they didn't give it much thought at the time the crime happened. Hearing a bump in the night may mean nothing to someone who lives near a crime scene, but it can be very important to me, trying to put the puzzle together.

We solve many more crimes than we don't solve, but it's the ones that get away that prey on our minds. So we don't get as much credit as we deserve – that's a part of the job you have to learn to live with. You have to know you gave every case the very best you could."

I Am a Homicide Detective in a Major City

"It's important to bring the right balance to this job. You have to be dauntless and persistent. You must have a passion for solving mysteries. At the same time you can't come at these cases with such a fervor that you jump to unfounded conclusions. Keeping your emotions in check is a very important part of the job. But some cases can get to you, and sometimes you might have to let another detective handle that case or at least be the lead detective in that investigation.

In murder cases, you have to develop a profile of who the victim was and who the killer is. These are people you know nothing about when your investigation begins. Naturally, it's easier to put a dossier together on the victim because you usually have the identity of that person – but not always. Sometimes you will be called to the scene of a murder where there will be no purse, no wallet, no cell phone, and no type of identification at all on or near the victim. When that happens, you start investigating the case not knowing who either the victim or the murderer is.

When you do know who the victim is, you can talk to people who knew that person. That person's life starts to come into focus. However, to determine who the perpetrator is, you have to begin by piecing together that person's profile, based solely on evidence at the crime scene and the way the crime was committed.

We rely heavily on witnesses to solve these cases. People always hear or see something. Sometimes they don't think it means anything. Other times they are afraid to come forward. But we can't solve any of these cases without the help of the public. That's why we canvass the neighborhood where a murder occurs to find anyone who can give us the slightest bit of information.

The biggest change in this field involves technology. Evidence of all kinds can be analyzed these days and that gives us leads we never had before, but it is not just the forensics. It's the digital footprint people leave behind with their cell phones and computers. We know who people communicated with and where they have been. This gives us insights that were never available years ago. That can be the lead we need to crack the case.

Every year we solve roughly 70 percent of the homicide cases we get. We also never stop looking at cold cases, and we solve many of those as well. Considering how little information we start out with on every case, that's pretty good. While the city I work in has about three hundred to four hundred murders a year, my precinct catches only about 15 to 20 of those. That's a lot of cases for a bureau to handle.

I don't know if people realize how much legwork is involved in solving these cases. We track down every lead and talk to everyone who knew the victim and, when we get a suspect, everyone who knew that person. We spend a great deal of time at the crime scene, trying to reenact what might have happened. We never give up on a case. The ones that go cold stay with us, so we want to solve those cases as much as the victims' families want them solved."

I Work As an Undercover Detective

"There is no more thrilling or dangerous job in law enforcement than working as an undercover detective. Working undercover is about playing a role and staying in character as long as you remain on that assignment. It involves assuming an identity to infiltrate a criminal organization. That means you use a different name in everyday life. All the identifying information in your wallet, including the driver's license and the credit cards you carry, are in that name. You even have a birth certificate in your assumed name and, just in case the criminals decide to check you out, an entire history is created for the person you are supposed to be. There will be credit reports and a work history in your assumed identity, a social security number, school records, and a criminal history, if needed. Most undercover detectives even have an apartment with a lease in their assumed name. You carry no police credentials and no badge. You don't carry a gun, either, unless the role you are playing requires it.

Undercover assignments can last anywhere from a few months to a few years, depending on how quickly you gain the confidence of people in the crime organization you are in and how fast you are gaining sensitive information.

Oftentimes, the person you are playing might be very different from who you really are, but before you take on this assignment, you learn about the criminals you will be mingling with. You and your law enforcement agency gather intelligence on them. Learning about the habits, families, background, likes and dislikes, and views of the people in the crime organization you will be infiltrating will allow you to develop a character that has a lot in common with these individuals. You will be able to assume their mannerisms, talk about the same things they do, and lull them into a sense of security, gaining their trust by forging a common bond with them. Undercover detectives have to completely fit in to the criminal groups they are sent to spy on.

This job requires a great deal of patience. Building relationships and gaining trust are not easy. There will always be someone who doesn't like you, sees you as an interloper, doesn't trust you, or feels threatened by you. An undercover detective has a handler in the law enforcement agency. The undercover detective reports to this handler periodically.

An undercover detective must have a great memory. A vital part of the job is being able to recollect everything you see going on in the lawbreaking operation you're infiltrating. Taking written notes is far too dangerous while you are actually working with these criminals. Gathering evidence surreptitiously is another major part of the job, and finding a safe drop-off point where you can leave that evidence for your handler to pick up is essential as well. Giving your handler information so police can conduct raids or make arrests has to be based on knowledge that anyone in the organization could have, so the tip can never be traced back to you.

Outwardly, you can have little contact with friends and relatives who know your real identity, for fear that you might have been followed and your cover will be blown. Undercover detectives are used when a criminal operation is so tightly run that there is no other way to get incriminating information and evidence about the lawbreakers unless it is collected from the inside."

PERSONAL QUALIFICATIONS

POLICE DETECTIVES AND CRIMINAL investigators have to be unrelenting. It takes endless hours of painstaking work going through clues, collecting evidence, reviewing computer records, following paper trails, talking to witnesses, and going over the crime in your mind countless times. This is not a job for a person who loses interest after taking a few quick looks at a file. Criminal investigators live with these cases day and night. They can never tire of checking out new leads or lose the desire to solve a crime, no matter how cold the trail becomes.

Crime busters are people with a strong sense of justice. They want to give crime victims and their families some type of closure and they want to make sure the right person is apprehended for the crime that was committed. Arresting the wrong person means the real criminal is still at large.

Having an eye for detail is a must when you investigate crimes for a living. You have to be able to juggle many cases at one time. That requires investigators to be extremely well organized. Files on every case you handle must be complete and easy for another detective to decipher. There is no room for sloppy work in this field. There is just too much at stake, and criminal investigators must be well aware of the impact their work has on people's lives.

The fainthearted need not apply. Crime scenes may be gruesome, and talking with victims and their family members is difficult and often heart-wrenching.

You must always remain impartial. Decisions have to be made based on the evidence and the facts. Even if you would like certain pieces of the puzzle to fit together in a particular way, you cannot do anything that will alter the evidence to have it show something that is false. This is a job where your character must be beyond reproach. Honesty is as vital in this career as the ability to pick up on key clues.

Critical-thinking and problem-solving skills are both elements of investigating crime and eventually cracking a case. A healthy dose of confidence does not hurt, either. Investigators have to believe, as they grow in this career, that the knowledge they gain from each case they work on keeps them one step ahead of the criminals.

Good writing and speaking communications skills help investigators maintain a rapport with everyone they work with, including colleagues in other law enforcement agencies, victims, witnesses, and even snitches and crooks who are willing to provide information about a crime they know or heard about. Police detectives have to write reports and give constant updates about cases they work.

A well-written report makes it easy to go back over a file and find what is needed quickly. Vague, incomplete, or poorly written reports serve no one and only slow down the process when those documents are looked up at a later date. People rarely think about writing skills when contemplating a career as a police detective or criminal investigator, but the ability to write clearly and concisely is appreciated not only by other investigators, but by prosecuting attorneys and others involved in the court system as well.

ATTRACTIVE FEATURES

BEING A CRIMINAL INVESTIGATOR IS A very rewarding job from a number of perspectives. Most importantly, you get to help people. Police detectives apprehend perpetrators who, in the course of their criminal activities, leave a trail of victims behind. These crooks care nothing about their victims. The only way victims can see justice done is if you collect evidence against the culprits, track them down, and make arrests.

At times you will recover items – sometimes family heirlooms – that were stolen from victims. On other occasions, you will capture a criminal who murdered someone and help bring closure to the victim's family. You serve as the voice for the voiceless in these cases. You are the one who represents the interests of victims in these difficult times, making sure criminals do not get away with it.

There is no better feeling than solving a crime and outsmarting a suspect. Lawbreakers never think they will be caught and often take a perverse pleasure in eluding the police.

Police detectives turn the tables on these fiends, figuring out their schemes and arresting them. It is a game of wits and sometimes nerves, as you reconstruct a crime and then out think the perpetrator and make a collar. Breaking a case takes intelligence, cunning, and creativity, all of which you showcase in this job.

Criminal investigators learn something from every case they work, and while no two cases are exactly alike, lessons you learn from one case will always help you on another case down the road. Nothing you learn in this job is wasted.

In large law enforcement agencies, like urban police departments, detectives can specialize in the investigative work they excel in, like solving homicides or robberies. This gives you an opportunity to hone your skills in one particular area.

Technology and science are your allies. In recent years, there have been numerous technological and scientific innovations that can help you with your investigations. Many of these breakthroughs are totally unknown to criminals, and that gives you the upper hand. New technology and scientific discoveries continue to keep the field of criminal investigation on the cutting edge of law enforcement.

You will never get bored in this job. The work is always varied and exciting. Some days you can barely catch your breath.

Criminal investigators are well respected in police departments and in the community. Many police detectives have become renowned for the major cases they have solved and the notorious criminals they have sent to jail. Police detectives are often invited to speak at community gatherings about crime prevention and methods of detection. This enhances the image of investigators in the community and in the country as a whole.

One of the perks of being a police detective is a nice pension that you can take after 20 to 25 years on the job. The pension gives you the opportunity to retire early enough in life to pursue another career, if you want, or a hobby you never had time for in the past.

A wonderful camaraderie develops in detective bureaus. As a police detective, you make some enduring friendships with people who understand the job and have a true passion for it.

UNATTRACTIVE ASPECTS

BEING A CRIMINAL INVESTIGATOR CAN BE a very stressful job, especially when you are grappling with a high-profile case that the public, the media, elected officials, and your superiors want solved quickly. Police detectives working in any size department can find themselves suddenly faced with intense pressure to clear a big case with speed and shrewd investigative work. Even if a case does not garner headlines, like a rash of break-ins in a local neighborhood, people affected by the crime spree want an arrest promptly.

You encounter frustration in this job and you cannot let it show. Following numerous tips that go nowhere is typical. If nothing turns up, you follow more clues until you get a break in the case. It can take days, weeks, months, or even years to get a solid lead in some cases, let alone arrest a suspect.

You deal with witnesses who are afraid to tell you everything they saw, even though you know they are holding back vital information that could make a difference in the case. You also come across people who are somehow involved in the crime, but, naturally, they refuse to talk to you or admit anything. Criminal investigators have to find a way around these stumbling blocks to get to the truth and solve the mystery.

In certain cases, crimes are committed but few clues are left behind and there are no witnesses. Nevertheless, it is up to you to use the few clues you do have to piece the puzzle together and track down the criminal.

Some crimes are never solved. Those cases can prey on a detective's mind, crying out for justice. In these cases you often feel as though you let the victim and the victim's family down, and you are constantly aware that the criminals involved in unsolved cases remain at large to hurt others.

Police detectives see a great deal of heartache, yet they have to look past it. A criminal investigator comes across the worst in humanity. It can test your faith in people and make you suspicious of most individuals and their motives for doing things.

Danger is part of this job. Nobody likes to be apprehended for committing a crime and you might be injured on the job in what seems to be the most harmless of situations.

At one point or another, all detectives have to testify in court. It is the job of the defense attorney to undermine your conclusions and tear your investigation apart. Such questioning can be infuriating, considering that you painstakingly put together evidence in the case before you made an arrest, and you are sure the suspect committed the crime.

One of the biggest disadvantages of the job is working odd hours. Police detectives do have regular work schedules but, at times, they have to work on weekends, holidays, and overnight. Regardless of their regular schedule, most police detectives are on call 24 hours a day and often get called in during off-hours.

Sometimes you will work a case way beyond the normal eight-hour workday most people are accustomed to. During a tough case you might have little time to sleep or spend with your family. However, you know going in that this is a demanding career that takes priority in your life.

EDUCATION AND TRAINING

MOST POLICE DEPARTMENTS AND LAW enforcement agencies around the country require only a high school diploma or a GED for new recruits. However, those with either a two-year associate degree or a four-year bachelor's degree in Criminal Justice, Police Science, Public Safety or a related field have an edge among job seekers in this field. A college degree will give you a better chance of landing a higher-paying job in a more prestigious law enforcement agency, advancing to the detective bureau in a police department faster, and reaching a supervisory position.

Education is valued in this field. The competition to get a job in any police department or law enforcement agency is tough. All things being equal, if it comes down to choosing a person with a high school diploma or a college degree for a job, the college graduate will win.

What getting a degree in Criminal Justice, Police Science, or Public Safety shows is that you took the time to learn something about the field and know what you are getting into. There is also the maturity factor that comes with spending several years studying for a college degree. Add to that a variety of recent studies, including one from Michigan State University that reveals that college-educated law enforcement officers are much less likely to use force on the job than officers who do not have higher education. That is one reason why law enforcement agencies are now hiring people with college degrees more than ever before.

Many community colleges offer two-year associate degrees in Criminal Justice that will help prepare you for a career as a criminal investigator. At Green River College in Auburn, Washington, for instance, courses in Criminal Evidence, Criminal Law, and Forensic Science make up part of the Criminal Justice curriculum. Bucks County Community College in Newtown,

Pennsylvania also offers a two-year associate degree program in Criminal Justice, with courses including Criminal Procedure, Criminal Investigation, and Terrorism Investigation.

Erie Community College (ECC) in Williamsville, New York has one of the many two-year Police Science programs found around the country. Police Administration, Basic Law for Police, and Criminology are some of the subjects at ECC. You are bound to find a community or junior college near you that offers programs similar to these.

An increasing number of four-year colleges have Criminal Justice programs. Some of these include the University of Wisconsin-Milwaukee; Temple University in Philadelphia; Utah Valley University in Orem, Utah; Loyola University in Chicago; and Indiana University in Bloomington, Indiana, among many others.

When it comes to Police Science, John Jay College of Criminal Justice in New York City has been a leader in the field for decades. Besides offering a bachelor's degree in Police Studies, the school has a four-year degree in Criminal Justice and even a master's degree and a doctorate in Criminal Justice. John Jay College also offers four-year degrees in a number of other public safety disciplines.

George Washington University, in the nation's capital, has an outstanding bachelor's degree program in Police and Security Studies. St. Mary's University of Minnesota is another college offering a four-year Police Science degree. Classes are offered at both the Twin Cities (Minneapolis) and Apple Valley campuses of St. Mary's University of Minnesota.

Law enforcement agencies also find that individuals with Psychology and Sociology degrees make good police detectives and criminal investigators because these courses of study focus on understanding people and their surroundings.

Whether you go to college or not, most police departments and law enforcement agencies around the country require that newly hired police officers with no experience on the job attend a police academy. These new recruits must successfully complete the academy course of study before serving on the job. This training can take between eight weeks and six months. There are no national criteria for how long the police training should last.

Many big city and large law enforcement agencies have their own police academies. Mid-size to small police departments send recruits to a regional police academy. Usually this training is paid for by the police department that hires you.

Police academy training can be intense and new recruits can flunk out of the program or fail the course of study when final grades are given out. Once you gain some on-the-job experience in a law enforcement agency, you have the opportunity to move up to police detective or criminal investigator. At that point you might be required to return to the police academy for some advanced training in criminal investigation work.

EARNINGS

AS A POLICE DETECTIVE OR CRIMINAL INVESTIGATOR, your salary will vary, depending on whether you work on the local, state, or federal level. On the local level, the size of the jurisdiction where you work – big city versus small town – also impacts the amount of your paycheck. Geographic location of your job has a great deal to do with your earnings as well.

The median national annual salary for police detectives and criminal investigators is about $75,000. But salaries are often lower than that in the nation's South, and higher in large urban areas in the Northern, Midwestern, and Western sections of the country.

For example, in New York City the average salary for a city police detective is about $95,000 a year. Salaries can go as high as $110,000, and even higher with overtime. In Chicago, police detective salaries range from $90,000 to $105,000 annually; in Los Angeles salaries are comparable.

However, in New Orleans, police detectives earn between $70,000 and $80,000 per year. The yearly income for a detective in the Charlotte, North Carolina Police Department is $65,000 to $72,000.

At the state level, the salary for detectives on a state police force also depends on what part of the country you work in. In the New York state police, the salary range for detectives is $90,000 to $100,000, while Michigan state police average $70,000 to $85,000; Florida state police, $60,000 to $80,000; and Mississippi state police, $45,000 to $65,000.

Federal criminal investigators earn between $95,000 and $160,000.

Annual salaries can increase a substantial amount, based on experience and rank. Sergeants in the detective bureau can earn as much as $7,000 more a year, and lieutenants can add $8,000 per year to their income. Commanding a detective or criminal investigation unit can boost your yearly paycheck by $10,000.

OPPORTUNITIES

WITH SECURITY ON THE MINDS OF most Americans today, it is no wonder that government experts predict that the job market for police detectives and criminal investigators will grow by as much as 15 percent over the next decade. The increase in detective positions is expected to take place throughout the country, with police departments both large and small, on the local, state, and federal level, adding personnel to safeguard the well--being of a growing population.

In addition, there is an increasing focus nationwide on police detectives and criminal investigators tracking would-be perpetrators of both domestic and international terrorism and stopping those individuals before an act of violence is carried out. That requires more investigators on staff than ever before, working to prevent attacks.

A healthy amount of turnover usually occurs on an annual basis as detectives reach retirement age or put in enough years of service to take their pensions. As a result, criminal investigator posts are opening up for police officers looking to get their detective's shield. While many government agencies are facing budgetary constraints, law enforcement is an area where money is being spent as taxpayers look to political leaders to do whatever is necessary to provide security for the community.

One key area of job growth in this field is among criminal investigators with superior detective skills who also have technology expertise. Technology is playing a greater role in both catching criminals and crime prevention, so the combination of investigative and technology ability will help any candidate interested in becoming a police detective.

Law enforcement agencies are also looking for people with experience in criminal investigation who have leadership abilities to command detective units and bureaus. As the number of detectives grows, so will the demand for superior officers to oversee investigative operations.

Law enforcement offers excellent opportunities for people with military experience. This one career truly values the training people receive in the armed services. Law enforcement agencies heavily recruit people who have served in any branch of the military.

You will find job openings for both men and women in criminal investigation, especially when it comes to undercover work. Police operatives working undercover have always been an integral part of criminal investigation, but undercover work has become even more important with the ever-increasing concerns about national security.

Protecting the homeland has become the job of law enforcement agencies on all levels. That difficult task usually falls to criminal investigators who must be able to develop local sources of information to identify suspicious behavior of any kind. Often, this type of work has to be done by police detectives and criminal investigators who are willing to go undercover and foil plots before an unsuspecting public ever becomes aware of these dangers.

GETTING STARTED

MOST CRIMINAL INVESTIGATORS START out as police officers, patrolling a beat either by car or on foot. The early years in a police officer's professional life are critical and often impact whether he or she will ever go on to become a detective.

When young police officers first join a department, they usually go through a probationary period, after which their performance on the job is evaluated by their superiors. Other experienced police officers also weigh in on a rookie's work in the field, and willingness to learn department procedures and make the adjustments needed to do the job well.

A number of factors are considered when superiors assess a police officer's first months on the job, including temperament, judgment, reaction to difficult on-the-job situations, reflexes, alertness, and whether you come to work every day ready to meet the challenges that lie ahead. This is not a job where you can coast.

Many young police officers get terminated either during the probationary period or right after it concludes. The length of the probationary period varies from department to department, but usually runs from nine months to a year. Some last as long as two years. This crucial time often sets the tone for how far you will go in this job.

If you make it through the probationary period, most law enforcement agencies require you to put in at least three or four years on patrol before you are considered for a position on the detective squad. Some police officers who want to be detectives work patrol much longer than three or four years, waiting for a vacancy to open up in their department's detective bureau.

So if you are determined to become a criminal investigator, you may want to check out the size of the detective bureaus in the police departments you are thinking of applying to and see if there is room for advancement in the time frame you would like. In addition, you might want to look into the requirements for becoming a criminal investigator in a federal law enforcement agency.

The time you spend on patrol is extremely valuable. You learn something every day that helps make you a better police officer and, eventually, a better detective when you land that post.

Experience counts in this job. Your superiors notice everything you do, like overhearing something in the crowd at a crime scene that can help tie up some loose ends in a case and reporting it to the investigating officers. That makes your stock go up.

Whatever you do that sets you apart from the other candidates is helpful in your quest to become a police detective. Some law enforcement agencies promote police officers to detective on merit, others give exams, some use a combination of both.

When it comes to making promotions to the detective bureau, all police departments strongly rely on the performance of police officers during their early years on the force. So use those years wisely and do not take them for granted. Your years on patrol are an important proving ground.

SCHOOLS

■ **Green River College**
http://www.greenriver.edu/academics/areas-of-study/details/criminal-justice.htm

■ **Bucks County Community College**
http://www.bucks.edu/academics/department/social-behavioral/criminal-justice

■ **Erie Community College**
https://www.ecc.edu/client/programdetail.aspx?ID=4075

■ **University of Wisconsin-Milwaukee**
http://uwm.edu/socialwelfare/academics/bs-in-criminal-justice

■ **Temple University**
http://bulletin.temple.edu/undergraduate/liberal-arts/criminal-justice/ba-criminal-justice

■ **Utah Valley University**
www.uvu.edu/catalog/current/departments/criminal-justice-law-enforcement/criminal-justice-bs

■ Loyola University Chicago
http://www.luc.edu/criminaljustice/undergraduate.shtml

■ Indiana University
www.indiana.edu/~crimjust/undergraduate_home.php?nav
=undergraduate

■ John Jay College of Criminal Justice
www.jjay.cuny.edu/academics-10

■ George Washington
Universityhttps://cps.gwu.edu/police-security
-studies

ASSOCIATIONS

■ Federal Criminal Investigators Association (FEDCIA)
http://www.fedcia.org

■ National Homicide Investigators Association
http://nationalhomicideinvestigators.org

■ Federal Law Enforcement Officers Association (FLEOA)
www.fleoa.org

■ National Association of Police Organizations (NAPO)
http://www.napo.org

■ International Association of Undercover Officers
http://www.undercover.org

■ Academy of Criminal Justice Sciences (ACJS)
www.acjs.org

PERIODICALS

■ POLICE Magazine
FBI Law Enforcement Bulletin
Law Officer
American Police Beat
Cops Today International
Police Chief Magazine
Law and Order

WEBSITES

■ **Law Enforcement Today**
www.lawenforcementtoday.com

■ **Association of State Criminal Investigative Agencies (ASCIA)**
https://www.ascia.org

■ **High Technology Crime Investigation Association (HTCIA)**
https://www.htcia.org

■ **PoliceOne**
http://www.policeone.com

■ **Officer**
http://www.officer.com

■ **The Society of Professional Investigators (SPI)**
http://spionline.org

■ **International Association of Crime Analysts (IACA)**
http://www.iaca.net

■ **Narcotic Enforcement Officers Association (NEOA)**
http://neoa.org

■ **The Detectives' Endowment Association (DEA)**
https://www.nycdetectives.org

■ **Police Foundation**
https://www.policefoundation.org/